PRAISE FOR *WOMAN PRIME*

Gail DiMaggio is a poet whose work is memory. She recasts the past so we begin to understand that the world actually has only two temperatures—love and fear: "Precisely. No bias or preference. Everything equal in its burning away." *Woman Prime* looks directly at the life of a daughter and wife and mother all the while showing us how silly it is to try and see our whole and complex existence without getting tears in our eyes. Heartfelt and headlong, this is a beautiful debut.

—Jericho Brown, poetry editor, *The Believer*

Gail Dimaggio's *Woman Prime* centers the female experience—marking the roles of daughter, sister, mother, lover, wife as invaluable and foundational. Part-ekphrasis, part-origin story, this debut collection unflinchingly examines a history of hurt: inflicted by those who pledged their love, and by the speaker herself. The ease with which DiMaggio slips in and out of the artworks she references—embodying the women and girls frozen in film or on canvas, reimagining their great hungers—might lead the reader to conflate theses intertwining narratives. However, these poems assert that a woman cannot be divided or diminished by anything other than herself.

—Emari DiGiorgio, author of *Girl Torpedo* and *The Things a Body Might Become*

With cheek to the gritty skin of the sidewalk perspective, Gail DiMaggio, in her debut collection *Woman Prime*, mines memory and masterpieces for reflection at the moment of recognition. She's familiar/ with disaster—a daughter lost to suicide. / Paintings a boyfriend cut from the frame/ to wrap the plumbing. Through the works of Alice Neel, Singer Sargent, Kahlo, de Koonig, Warhol, and through a collage of family history, DiMaggio painstakingly restores relentless beauty with sensuous honesty. In the poem, "Maybe They Will Drown Him," after Willem de Koonig's *Clam Diggers,* Two women up to their calves / in wave surge, painted small as if framed/ in a side-view mirror and closer/ than they look, the feast quickly turns from devour to destroy as DiMaggio exposes seduction and its many betrayals. And though the title poem riffs on de Koonig's, *Woman I*—a rendering of the power and danger of the feminine—the collection also considers the other definition of prime, the divisibility of one by one, a notion found in the poem, "We Are Always Falling Forward," where, someday Tony will turn his/ blinded face from me and say: Look,/ what I have done to myself. The view, even when seen through a "him" remains ultimately hers. Though he will hold her down, or paint her monster-sized breasts; what reflects remains both undeniable and insatiable.

—Ann Dernier, author of *In the Fury*

Woman Prime

Woman
Prime

GAIL C. DIMAGGIO

Text © 2018 University of Alaska Press

Published by
University of Alaska Press
P.O. Box 756240
Fairbanks, AK 99775-6240

Cover and interior design by Jen Gunderson, 590 Design

Cover art: *Radius*. © 2017 Helen Frankenthaler Foundation, Inc. /
Artists Rights Society (ARS), New York / Tyler Graphics Ltd., Mount
Kisco, New York

Library of Congress Cataloging-in-Publication Data
Names: DiMaggio, Gail, author.
Title: Woman prime / by Gail DiMaggio.
Description: Fairbanks, AK : University of Alaska Press, [2018] |
Identifiers: LCCN 2017031742 (print) | LCCN 2017042164 (ebook) |
    ISBN 9781602233430 (ebook) | ISBN 9781602233423 (softcover :
    acid free paper)
Classification: LCC PS3604.I4638 (ebook) | LCC PS3604.I4638 A6
    2018 (print) | DDC 811/.6dc23
LC record available at https://lccn.loc.gov/2017031742

For Tony

CONTENTS

DEFIANCE
IN
GIRLS

A naked imp, hands on her hips, black hair
crackling with curls, cleft chin tilted while
she calculates a breakout. She could say *fuck.*

She could kick glass out of the French door. I did once.
Tore the dress from its hanger, got tar
on my new shoes and would not cry, would not

cry when my mother hit me with a stick.
Isabetta stares into the eyes of the artist
who is her mother. Who believes

she can make this child again. Make her over.
Can capture that long throat, the hand
like a skylark's claw. When I told my own girl:

Do not cut your hair,
she chopped it off in handfuls. Someday
Isabetta will dance a made-up dance for her father,

try a little coke for a lover. But here,
in this north light, she faces her mother
who sees things in her—some of them true,

but already changing. I've walked a long beach
in deep fog, my hands filled with shards.
Girl shrapnel.

After Alice Neel, *Isabetta,* 1935

1

BLOOD RELATIONS

I am wishbone, nude
and gnawed on. They've left me
broken off sharp. Once I was
a tender place in the throat.

He is knife blade,
keen to slice and sliver.
What can the starving do,
but love him?

She is plum, bitter skin
and sour flesh. Whoever rends her
will be fed. At the core, she holds the pit.
Buried, she erupts.

MY
FATHER
SAID
HE'D
TEACH
ME

I admit to blank spots. Certain facts appear—
disappear. The cucumber vine shackling my ankle—
sometimes it's loaded with yellow crepe-paper buds. Not yet fruit.
Sometimes I stroll into the sodden garden,
other times I crawl and my knees bleed
from shards of gravel. I remember
the seashell pattern in my mother's dress, her caramel smell,
but not always the groveling, or the certainty
that from his high windows my father sees me
scrabbling on my belly. People ask about him,
about why he did or didn't. There are vivid
colors. There are absences. I see
his mouth move. I see the dark zero swing
my way. Maybe he says: or you'll wish you had.
A neighbor pushes fabric
under the sewing needle, a kid passes the gate
eyes down for sidewalk cracks. My mother says:
All the lights were red, that's why.
If I pressed my arms to my chest
it was out of love for my own flesh, my own pounding heart.
When my father's aim tore earth and not my body,
I loved him.

After Danielle Deulen, "Interrogation"

FOUNDATION

My mother wasn't supposed to wear it.
Daddy said: You are more beautiful

bare faced. What
are you trying to hide? So the first secret

was the clam-shaped compact
and its icy sponge. Sometimes, it's morning—

sometimes December—and she calls me
to the bathroom, case open,

water running. I dream
her oval face, the mirror watching—

and the way we are afraid.
She wipes foundation on my left cheek, above

my collar, down my right arm, left
wrist. The cold stiffens

at my throat, the garland
of his finger marks wanes, and the mirror-face

lifts her chin and promises:
I will live in a casket of ivory beige, and be

her good girl.

GIRLS

IN

PICTURES

Flora's the one who stands
closest to the dark, arms limp, eyes
turned from the vigilant mother
who leans close to the artist,

and whispers. I used to try
to capture my daughter, Lisa,
in photographs. In this one, you might see
a girl, laughing

instead of the girl who's done
with testifying to our happiness, the girl
who spun to face me, arms out,
shouting: Is this what you want? Is it?

I thought it was. What I wanted.
To celebrate menarche,
I had Lisa's ears pierced and bought
gold knots to gleam in her dark curls. She

hated them—hated the struggle
to find the opening, force the post through.
In this photograph, sunset
gilds her face. She's watching

horses pass and return.
Muscled and dusty—
stallion's haunch, mare's curved neck.
Their hooves are stamping out a drumbeat.

It makes the ground shiver.

After John Singer Sargent,
The Daughters of Edward Darley Boit, 1882

ONE
GOOD
FRIDAY

Twelve jazz men here to rile Assumption Parish
       and every god who hates a raucous prayer.
In white boots and short red skirt,

I'm half asleep on the evening steps
       and a dog pack of clouds
is tracking the moon. I light a Marlboro

and wait to touch you.
       Suddenly, Bruce's voice:
Good Moroccan goddamn hash,

You swing me close, then across the lot,
       and my hand slaps flat on the van's flank.
Miles of dark and a bumpy road.

Richie says: Christ, we're in some cemetery.
       A stone angel spins past
and Don—unsteady with his flute—stands

through the open roof to send a rapture
       in B-flat through the hemlock feathers
into the streaming clouds. Now in a room

patched with moonlight, a clock
       blinks a neon three,
and my boot lies broken ankled

where I tossed it to the carpet.
       I am thirsty
for the hollow at the base of your throat.

Your hand on my thigh,
       your mouth on my breast,
you wake me.

RING SONG

This same swift brightness—
I've seen it on silver guppies
cupped in my brother's
hands. In a chick's underwing
tickled by the wind. In the *four
and twenty blackbirds*
children sing at morning recess.
Their *pocket full of posies,
their all fall down.*
            In every kind of
falling down:
dominoes and Pisa's tower,
the sunny blur
when my Christmas bike
skidded out. In tinfoil
tiaras, and a whole blue sky
for a single cloud
            gold as the braid
on Dad's navy hat. Swift
as Ma's needle
rattling into the sheen of satin,
and I've seen it in the satin dress I wore
the night I didn't sleep
with Bob—how I wanted to—and in
            the trumpet
on *Lush Life*, the fiddle
on *Orange Blossom Express.*
In a jazz score
laid out under the hanging lamp—
with your hand, love,
making neat, black strokes:
quarter note, whole note,
half note.
            Rest.

BEWILDERED

Route 30 will take us to the right lake,
the one where we have reservations
and hope of sleep. Once, I had to choose—

driver? navigator? Today I'm both.
The kids know. They whisper and pinch each other.
We have fuel, I tell them. We have

light in the sky. Far behind me now
the last house and nobody watching
from any window. The wilderness arrives

threaded with paths, pockmarked
with boulders like a landed spaceship
or the skull of triceratops. My oldest

sees a twelve-point buck step
from the trees. The youngest sees a cave
and in it, a dragon

with scales like black glass,
and blind, white eyes. This is
north country. Here travelers

lose themselves, leave the known route
for a nameless track
headed into a mutter of rapids.

Water, if we could reach it,
and all of us thirsty.

MAYBE
THEY
WILL
DROWN
HIM

They are so naked. Skin a northern pale,
hair blonde and tangled. Some sag to the breasts.
Two women up to their calves
in wave surge, painted small as if framed

in a side-view mirror and closer
than they look. His brush strokes a thigh, a hip,
and there they stand, wavering
in the moon's push. In the ocean's pull. Once

he was a boy in his mother's kitchen,
her buxom shape loomed in the window,
and he learned to flinch and duck.
That woman packed a roundhouse right.

Maybe they will drown him
in Atlantic pleasure. Maybe
he will take them home,
the three of them, up all night, feasting. Two women

who cock plump hips
to lure him. Two women dissolving
in salt spray, breaking up
in sunshine like a bad radio signal. Olives and

oysters and lemon.
Their hands on his muscled back, his
on a sweet, round breast.
The sliding down. The going under.

After Willem de Kooning, *Clam Diggers,* 1963

COLD
THURSDAY

Stopped in the frame of the kitchen doorway
you hold up the button fallen
from your worn cuff, and tell me:

Go to Walmart, I need—
but our daughter is reading out a question:
What goddess tried to save

her drowning husband?
You tell her: That wouldn't be
your mother. You need mending

and aspirin, I need salt, and Lisa
is studying the story of a woman
who—over and over—failed

to rescue the man she loved.
Are you angry that you're late for the gig,
that I'm doing her homework. Am I angry

that when you spot the row of photographs
hung above the stairs, you call them
The Happy Family Display?

You carry your horn down the driveway at dusk.
I need olives and cold nights,
a spool of white cotton thread,

and a wilder heart. Lisa wakes sobbing:
Spiders, Mommy, in the cupboard.
I scrub every corner with hot water,

with bleach. My fingers go numb.
I leave a note on your pillow:
Don't wake me.

FRIDA'S
HAIR

How is a woman's life anchored if not
by the weight of a man on top of her? I've felt

the jolt as the lines let go, the sudden drift
and pointlessness. Each of us loved a man

who loved our hair—and under the cascade, naked breasts.
But other women had curls as wild, flesh as sleek

without Frida's gull-wing brow, or my
quacking voice. Without my habit of opinions, hers

of taking his canvas to paint her own face.
Frida has cropped her hair. Hanks of it

crawl toward a dawn sky
radioactive and empty.

I think I will keep my hair,
but I'm ready to put on the fat man's suit,

the red shirt. Spread my legs wide
and hold the shears close to my crotch at a threatening angle.

I know what it feels like to want the man afraid.
To imagine the blade

slicing a bright, excruciating line
down somebody's inner thigh.

After Frida Kahlo, *Self-Portrait with Cropped Hair,* 1940

MY FATHER SAID
HE'D MAKE A KNIFE

He's under the floors in his stone room, master
of sharp tools and cutting. I stand four feet back

exactly where he tells me while he slips
a slat into the vice, spins the handle,

tightens the jaws. My hand
gestures after his in the heated air.

In his fist, suddenly, his belt. He jerks it
till the brass tongue springs free, and the supple

length hisses from the loops,
till the buckle's nestling in his palm.

How often, really? I ask, cradling
my newborn, and my sister snaps: All the time.

Once, he made a crooked wooden bowl, like
the broken half of a sparrow's egg.

I am almost twelve when he boasts
he'll make a knife, and the snarl

of the sharpener haunts the house. But when the blade
drops and he tries to snatch it out of the air,

it slices through three fingertips. His footsteps
take the stairs one and one,

like a monster in a movie. His hand
cradles his hand, red spills over his palms,

to bloom on the black tile, bloom again on
the white, and I watch and watch his blood

spreading on the checkerboard floor.

NIGHT

1. Time of darkness. The hours after the doctor's mouth moved, the black wave poured in, the void opened at my feet. And everyone certain I would cope. As in the neighbor: Oh, honey, everything will probably be fine in the morning. 2. The hours of no light, no garage door opening, no car purring in, no phone call, no girl's voice tinny with distance and excuses. 3. The last hours of the day, the hours always *after*. After work, after the highway and the argument, after he and I promised each other we'd survive, and, all right, I did, but first—blood draws, sunset, sunset, the smell of prayers. 4. In a Bruegel painting, Truth holds the chain and Night sprawls—bare-breasted, fanged, feeding on the tongues of the damned. As in: Look what the night has carved into my face. **Related Word:** Nightfall. The long, slow sobs of the man I failed to comfort, the bed shaking under him so I slept in another room, so I turned on every lamp, so I drove to the river or a lover or a casino, played the running numbers, pumped my hips to the hard, hard rock, and Night waited, patient and inevitable, rubbing her furry haunch against the door.

YOU,
MARILYN,
FIVE DEEP,
TEN ACROSS

I love your head scarf, Number Four,
also, your citrine hair. Nights,
killing time online, I guess
at your weight and watch you work the crowd
outside the Ritz in '59. All that talent

for childlike, for breasts, for a flash of thigh
sliding the hot seat of the limousine. And I love you both,
Fifty and Twenty-five. One so pale, the other so black.
Made from a photo taken on that all-day shoot—
publicity guys in your hotel room,

and you plump with early pregnancy.
The camera snout prods. You
perform: sunny and complicit
on the couch, belly down
on the bed. Staring up, deadpan,

into the bald glass of the lens.
Which of you looked back?
The one who slept with Jack? Then Bobby?
The one on the bungalow floor?
Or you, here at the end, so snow white.

After Andy Warhol, *Marilyn Diptych,* 1962

BROTHER
WOLF

I wondered if you knew that the Tropic of Cancer
drifts south half an arc second every year,
and if you could tell me the meaning

of that phrase: arc second? In tenth grade
you were the boy who wrote
an essay on *Lupercal*—blood

on the altar stones, a terrible
shrieking of goats, everyone
naked and running. Once I stole

your allowance and when you told Daddy,
he blacked my eye for starting trouble,
slapped you twice for whining.

So later in the dark, I burned
your homework in the woodstove.
You and I learned together how solid ground

is always slipping southward
toward some edge. We heard the blows
land. We heard our mother,

silent in the other room. This
is what I've salvaged: You were the one
who couldn't watch when Daddy

laddered my arm with bruises. I was the one
who left the room when he whipped you
with a willow switch.

HIDE-AND-GO-SEEK

There is a smell of wet wool,
my mother's face is a pale bird
against the ceiling,

and my father says he has had
enough. My throat aches
the way it always does

when he has had enough.
Blue stones—cold as the riverbed,
and I would give them back,

but they come spilling
out of my pockets, making
a death-rattle sound on the floor.

I am small, now,
smaller than I remember. I have
a splinter in my foot, and I never

hear the door
when it closes behind them.
Mommy, I try to call. *Daddy*.

My voice makes a sound
like tinder breaking.

EMPTY ROOM
WITH MOTHER
AND DAUGHTER

A '70's house, ice-blue slider
closed against the summer-green world. Sun
squared and triangled on the rug. I, too, once wore

pink tees and pale jeans, had hair like
Morgan le Fay, parted in the center. I, too, dressed
a baby girl in white with lace—

the soft-bristle brush, the tender curls. And then
the rest of the day. The rest of the next. My mother
bringing Pampers, rectangular

and antiseptic. This baby's hands
fist and punch—maybe this was the day
she got her third earache. But the painted woman's face

stays blank, her eyes fixed on sun shapes
pinned to the rug like a jigsaw
she needs to solve. Dacron

wedding dress, bay window at night,
streetlights blue on her long
thighs. The dark column of his throat.

Standing in the pantry breaking every dish.
When I told my mother
I didn't know what to do to soothe the pain,

she said: Get used to it.

After Alice Neel, *Ginny and Elizabeth,* 1976

MARRIED LOVE.
A TAXONOMY

Madison and Forty-Second, the city bus
pulls even with the library steps,
with a line of young trees
that might be linden—Tony,
master of the seed catalog,
would know, but he's
in Connecticut, and not in the mood
for botanicals—first it's one
anniversary then a dozen,
his friend Mike calls
drunk at two a.m. and I'm the one
who wakes for the phone, my mother
dying, and Tony won't
forgive what I said so how
do I forgive him, and the chatty
woman, my seatmate, leans into me
so I turn away toward the spiky tree,
its bristle of flowers.
        There's a girl—
cloud of dark curls, sprigged dress,
her dancer's body and lifted mouth,
offered to the boy

who stands before her,
hands at his sides. The line
of his body mirrors
the angle of hers. Open lips so close
they breathe each other's air.
　　　My heart slams
one arrhythmic beat into my ribs
wanting what she has,
what maybe I had
in the dank bed where we lie
sticky with sweat and sex, sheets
flecked with pumpkin seed—
they obsessed us, those seeds,
cheap and salty for the broke and in love.
　　　Another dozen years, we drive together
into the Superstitions and after we've laughed
at the cattle-guard rumbling under our wheels,
I lean into the yaw
of the switchbacks,
and remember
the girl under the linden
just before the kiss.

WE
ARE
ALWAYS
FALLING
FORWARD

July is a green pulse
pulling me outside where the lettuce
has bolted, where a blue
jay shrills its one word, *weep*,
and in the near woods,
the raccoons are sleeping
who will come tonight
to rape the ripe corn.
The screen door
slams. Tony's coming with Lisa
who calls, *Something, something, Mommy*,
and I say, *Um hmm*, and she runs
across the street for Billy Franco.
While I pluck fat, green tomato worms,
drown them in kerosene, Billy
holds the stakes, Tony hammers
them home, and we all laugh
when the jays dive-bomb the cats,
launching blue selves from the oak.
Noon sun, no shadows.
I herd the kids inside. Quartered tomatoes
drip scarlet on the Formica
and the olive oil my mother
brought from San Gimignano,
I pour it out—
lavish, generous—
and someday Lisa will follow
the wrong man south—Florida,
Texas, account disconnected—
and someday Billy's voices will whisper:
Razor. Will whisper: Running water,
and someday Tony will turn his
blinded face from me and say: Look,
what I have done to myself.

SOON
NOW

1. An unspecified future when all of today's dreary details vanish—no fights about his drinking, no credit card blues, no squeal in the rear axle, and now at last, her father holds her close and weeps for his cruelty. Out in the driveway—a shiny new car. On the soundtrack: Beethoven's Fifth. 2. A day of reckoning. As in: Soon now, he'll get what's coming to him: black eye, slow leak in a heart valve. Or it's a day of fulfillment and the children return to sit at the table. What a wonderful childhood, they will say. And no one will mention the belt or the shouting. 3. **Philosophical corollary.** Kant warns that *soon now* can never arrive. Heartbreak arrives and the news that the polar caps are melting. Old age. But never this jubilant *soon*, never this brilliant *now*. And that murmuration taking wing on the other side of the orchard? Those birds carry yesterday, a charred branch in their talons.

EN ROUTE,
1995

Afraid of a spring storm on its way to the canyon,
we flee downhill to Flagstaff
where CNN is breaking the Oklahoma City bombing—

striated rubble, gray dust. The building
before. The building after.
And Court TV's showing the front gate to OJ's house—

flagstones rippled with blood.
My husband holds my coffee
and I lean my head between the narrow wings

of the wall phone. It's my sister, Lenore.
Her mechanized voice jagged in the air.
Off her meds, he mutters. We are sure

we are helpless. We watch *Nightline*,
then *CBS This Morning*, and someone
in the café turns up the volume.

Nicole said, I wanted to be a wonderful wife,
but who can love a woman emptied out on the stones?
The lobby shop sells calendars—

the year in Byzantine icons. The Virgin
and Child, look across the sales floor
as if they would meet my eyes. It's Sunday,

everyone is watching
OJ squeeze his hand into that glove,
or the fireman with the dead child, blood

matted in her hair, spattered on her socks.
Her legs sprawl—like my little girl's
when we carried her upstairs asleep.

CASSANDRA
AND
ME

we see things coming—short sale,
Troy on fire, ex-wife
testing the ax's edge
on the pad of her thumb, but then
the tower burned anyway, and my child married
a man with a warrant out and Jack
Daniels in the glove compartment.
She told me she was afraid
I'd talk her out of it—
out of the turquoise loafers,
the house too near the bridge,
out of the man who stole
her phone or the one who left her
on the two a.m. street,
as if I've showed her the tarot card—
and suddenly she's backing
that wrecked Pinto down the driveway,
top speed, gears grinding because
she'd rather not be saved
if it's me who does the saving.
I dream the world
of if-only-she-would-listen:
no midnight hospital, no
miscarriage, no me suffering
the story of the miscarriage, me
marooned in this house where
if I close my eyes I can see her—
pigtailed, nine—helping her father
drive nails into the wallboard.

DEAN
AND
LINDA
IN A
CAR

In dirt-creased jeans her legs stretch
        through the open door of the car—
                some American make. Maverick?

Marauder? He's pulled it over, right-angled to the road and
        fuck the cop who tickets him.
                Behind her on the bench seat,

he swamps her shoulders with his meaty arms,
        locks one hand on the wrist of the other,
                bends his bearded face

to the back of her neck. He'll keep her safe.
        He'll keep her. And she
                has fitted herself backward

into the cup of his body. He probably likes his engines loud
        and faster than a Corsair. Maybe, she dreams
                a Vega and her own bedtime story—

stallion trapped in the corral, a house with its own
        refrigerator. Skylark, she loves him.
                Voyager, she forgets he's there.

Her pale eyes look out blank as steel.
        A Firebird.
                A Nova.

After Mary Ellen Mark, *The Damm Family in Their Car,* 1987

ALMOST THE FOURTH, 1980

Heading for the edge of the solar system—
Voyager I is filled with *The Sounds of Earth*:
a baby laughing, the call of whales. On East Lake Road,

my husband builds a blaze meant to burn down,
and I magnet another list
to my refrigerator. The Miami cop who cracked

a black man's skull has just been found
not guilty, and my father begins
another story: Some jungle

bunny, he says, and I hurry a nephew into grace.
For these and all thy gifts. The salad.
The salt. I rise to my feet with Amen.

Later, women at the sink, men
dismembering six packs, talking
brutal sergeants, drunken nights, Richard Pryor

soaked in rum, carrying catastrophe
forward on his own back. *Voyager I*
passes Saturn singing

the music of Mozart and our daughter,
high on fresh mowed grass,
sails down the yard, arms spread for wings.

Before I can notice,
dusk erases the little pear tree,
Voyager escapes the sun,

and my husband stands alone at the lot's edge
nursing his high. On the stone steps,
I pull a baby into my lap,

call out to the other children: Look up,
look up at the fireworks
blooming in the night sky.

WAIT
FOR
IT

A woman arrives at the pearly gates,
and she may be a whore, or somebody's mother, demented.
Or she comes across a carnival, gets lost in the hall of mirrors.

A woman strolls into a bar,
sees her own face in the mirror, and when
the barkeep asks, Bourbon shots? she says,

You know me very well. She sips, he polishes.
A daughter walks into a hall of mirrors
looking for her mother.

Or a mother who might be a witch,
might be a reflection in silvered glass,
walks into a bar on her way to the pearly gates,

and St. Peter pours her a shot. Or she's in a room
where nothing has changed—crib—window, two a.m.,
a crying child who—twenty years later—will say:

Please, Mom, I'll never ask again.
Mirror-woman's forehead warps into a long, upward plane.
Yeah, St. Bartender says, you always did overthink it.

And now she remembers how it goes—
the fun house, the gate, the bartender folding wings
and turning off lights.

LIGHT

1. That which makes everything visible. As in sunlight, as in lightning, as in the smile of the boy who approached her on the beach. And then she saw he was reaching for someone else. 2. Primary agent of vision and revision, bearer of blinding truth. As in, two a.m. headlights sweep the bedroom ceiling and now she knows that someday she will die. 3. *Adjective*—not dark: the room where she waited was filled with light, and still the news they brought required words like *already septic*. Afterward, she turned her eyes from even shuttered windows. Because Rumi can say the wound is the place where the light will enter us, but who wouldn't rather be contained in brightness than contain it? 4. *Verb*. To illuminate. And to ignite. To flame at the core of the furnace like molten glass, like that pinpoint sear when the laser pierces flesh, seeks marrow. Precisely. No bias or preference. Everything equal in its burning away.

WHAT
TO
DO IN
THE
DARK, I

Keep these items in a kitchen drawer: dull shears, your mother's lapis ring, three coins from a country you won't see again.

Tell about your father dying on a gurney by the ambulance bay, the giant door slamming open, thundering shut, and you were fascinated

by a stranger leaning on the wall, dried blood like a star on his face.

Tell about that dream where you're surrounded by animals, and a bear leans toward you, says: *Hey, Wolf, that woman mask doesn't fool me.*

Keep a list of things you've lost—the sound of your brother's voice, the swing in the maple tree, every spiral nebula.

Tell about the Gravely—how it ripped the rabbit's nest, killed the mother, sliced the litter, and your husband carried in the one survivor, asked you to save it.

Lush Life. Norwegian Wood. He loved sad tunes.

I STAYED

because my mother taught me
divorce is for women who can't
sing lullabies, and the upstairs neighbor

would say she was sorry, and did we try counseling.
Besides, I asked myself, What's so bad
about ordinary? Side by side

on the sofa, TV muted, no beer cans
in sight? And that time
he dragged in the Christmas tree

singing the "Work Song" from Snow White.
I stayed through the year of accusation—
where were you going did you fuck

just tell me did you did you?
I kept imagining a woman
in her own house, light

from the north, books scattered
on a scarred table, no one to care
that she stands at the window

talking aloud to herself. And I stayed
because, more often than not, I loved him,
though what I meant by love

kept changing—the sound
of his car in the driveway, the long
narrow bones of his hand, another

heartbeat in the winter bedroom.

WOMAN
PRIME

Years, he dragged cracked slabs
from the dream well. Shaped me
with hips like tectonic plates, Frisbee eyes

spinning. Outside his loft—day then night,
winter then winter, fools and a city
chewing on its own leg

while he drank and was faithful.
Painting and scraping, he unburied me,
his earthen goddess—first mother, last lover—

and offered me his wonder and disgust.
I loved him—for my Percheron hooves, my giant
strappy shoes rooted in dirt.

Bone shards and broken sticks fill my lap—
he wouldn't trust me with hands after
that night he took three fingers neat

and a hawk flew out of my mouth,
my flaccid, mountainous breast
whapped him in the face. He saw

these pretty lipstick lips can mimic
death's fat grin. But still, he made me
from the heron and the songbird,

from a severed hand advancing in gangrene,
a door, closing. Along its bottom edge—
a spring-green glimpse. Water.

After Willem de Kooning, *Woman I,* 1952

I CAN
HEAR
THE
NIGHT
TRAIN

coming at me across some August, making the prairie growl under my feet. First, it's a rumble, and then it's a rocking crowd, and Axel's an antic figure in a porkpie hat bellowing into his mike: Fly like an airplane. Feel like a space brain. The oncoming roar's a warning: step back, step away. Lower your goddamn voice or I'll spin you naked, snap your elbows out of joint. But I'm no de Kooning, the El keening in his ears while he paints his goddess with the monster boobs. When my husband freewheeled the car into a switchback on Beartooth Pass, and the speed drove silt into our eyes, I covered my face. But he loved it, loved the shrilling at the half-open window. Can you hear it? He could hear it—an E string vibrato that shreds the night and taunts the sleepers for a thousand miles.

THE
DESERT
ON
SUNDAY

Alive, you took more than your share of the bed.
  A hungry weight—
      always driving me closer to the edge.

We called that passion.

The surgeon slapped
    pale hands around your calf, said:
We'll cut the leg here. Right here,
    and I hated him.

    Should I make a list—
people to call, things to buy?
    One leg. So we buy one shoe?

    The green line peaked and valleyed.
In that small, white room—weight
    married silence and I

        looked to the surgeon for permission—

    Can I leave the room now?
        No?
            Ok, not now,
but soon—right?

NOBODY

can hear God, who goes on
unwinding the world,
not worried, apparently,

that none of us agree on his motives—
not the priest, not the infidel,
not the mother with her newborn.

I was a mother once. In a dim nursery,
at two a.m. the baby
refused the breast and

refused the breast, till I pleaded:
Look, God, don't you
want her to live? And as usual

Nobody answered. The moon went on
not shining in the night sky,
and the monk seal remained extinct.

So maybe, I thought,
maybe not a Word, but a Thing—
a heart-shaped stone

and I began to walk
with my eyes on the ground.
But when my husband refused

to rise from the dead
though I begged him, weeping,
Someone walked behind me,

turning off lights.
Yesterday, in a blue-black sky
dawn drew a line

sharp as a knife to the eye.
No one can tell me
such things speak for God.

No one can tell me they don't.

RADIUS II

Whatever she expects, the road ends here.
      Call it a snowfield. Call it a sheet of handmade paper
            crafted in the Japanese style. No hints or footprints,

not even a gentle slough where she might imagine
      a path going on under the surface. Just
            this icy white where

she wanders, rummages, stumbles
      across a block of heartwood—
            insect-drilled. And ringed—

one circle for every year of a life. It's as if she's staring
      into the eye of a hunting owl. For a long time,
            she sands against the grain,

thinks about a cobra's cowl and God's
      fingerprint, then gives it to the press. Iron
            bites wood, collisions pound out

a circle of trees, a black ocean,
      a red disk like the moon
            on Kepler 10b, or a bleed

at the back of the eye. Just one corner stays white. Peeled
      and flattened birch bark. A December field
            under new snow.

After Helen Frankenthaler, *Radius,* 1993

LIKE FLIGHT

Cross two states, five decades, the Gold Star
     Bridge. Dodge lanes of '67 Chevrolet-rumble
         and climb thirty-two concrete steps

to the hunchback house
     hugging its darkness. The swing still hangs
         in the side yard. First, grip

the rope, then step one foot up and push out hard.
     Hands and thighs, back and calves,
         knee-bend, knee-bend, using your weight

to force your weight up the arc,
     and up the arc until the rope
         goes slack and gravity

opens its hands. Now can you see the crooked yard,
     the house with its blind windows?
         And—across the road,

almost to the bridge—a girl, walking away.

PANAMA
SAILOR
BOY

I knew my father. His hand a weight
on the top of my head. His khakis stiff with starch.
　　If I gave him backtalk, he'd fish
　　　　　　　the spoon from the salad bowl,
crack me across the back of the head.

Dear Mamma and Papa,
　　This is the fifth day of rain here.　Dear Trank, I'll tell you
where I used to fish　　for bullheads.

But I never knew
　　　　　the letter-writing boy, the left-behind boy
　　who maybe got trapped in seaweed
　　　　　　off the Great Barrier Reef. *You should start,*
at the end of Mirror Lake, then walk west and go over
　　　　　　under the mountain.

　　　　　　When I was twelve, he described
a hull breach. A shipmate behind him, injured or
　　　　　just slow, my father slamming the hatch,
　　spinning the handle tight.
　　　　It was a standing order,　　he told us:
Save the ship.　　Leave the drowning behind.

　　Dear Trank,　　It's raining again. Remember—
　　　it gets dark fast up there. The mountain
watching.

Radar's vampire fingers
probe the water—and my father crouches
                    inside the coffin shape, inside
the deadly, exploding rain.

Dear Lee, it's raining hard now,
        and I'm writing to say
            I think of you.

Maybe the boy I never met
                turned to ivory on the Pacific floor.
Maybe he drifts   face downward,
        circled by tiny fish,
                by bits of broken sunset. *Over under the mountain.*
                At the end
                    of mirror lake.

Note: Nineteen and stationed in the Canal Zone, my father wrote
letters to his parents; his brother Trank, eleven; and his sister Lee,
sixteen. She saved them, envelopes and all, in a carved box he'd sent
her from Panama. The words in italics are taken from those letters.

TO THE CLOCK
I INHERITED
WHEN
MY FATHER
DIED

I've hung your darkness

on my white wall,
so each new day
can see itself warped

in wavering glass.
August green,
December white—

all the same to you.
Now, you say
and say again. *Now.*

OCTOBER
TRESPASS

I squeeze between "Closed Bridge" signs, pause
to look down at the bank where a guy in a red jacket

is showing his daughter how to hold
a fishing rod, pull it back and cast, her hands

swamped in his. When the line flies back
and floats to a landing, I hear them laugh together.

In the news this Sunday morning—Aleppo.
Also, a Manhattan woman who believed

in the elevator, stepped forward
and lost her daughter to gravity. She was

innocent, that mother. I wish I could tell her so—
but I'm a stranger on the other side

of two states, a river, a forest of pine. I swear
I never prayed to the great funnel of the sky

to keep me safe and far from the edge
of elevator shafts, bomb craters. What's prayer,

but a whisper in the mind stream,
an old habit. What my mother said.

The good father spots me, considers
my trespass without much interest, kneels

to zip his daughter's jacket.
From this half-finished place,

some of my suffering behind me,
no one left to call my name in the night,

I will pray into the emptiness
for the girl fishing, for the fish on its way

to her hook. For good fathers,
grieving mothers, the child falling,

and the child asleep
next to the bombed-out wall.

LIGHTNING

1. Bright, random lines that turn the night sky to a glass bell, crazed, about to shatter. Behind the dark—a wilderness of light. 2. **Related phrase**: lightning bolt, a jagged shaft that sparks the house, leaves the door charred and smoking. Transforms the afternoon. As in: she looked for the first time into the calm distance of her newborn's eyes. 3. Sometimes lightning forms a chain: After the diagnosis, she laid her hand on his thigh and could not lift it away. 4. But sometimes it's a globe—blue, luminous, close to the ground: Sitting by the window, she felt a flash of gratitude for coffee, for August dusk, for notes she'd made at twenty in the margins of *Walden*, and here they are again, ignorant and eager. 5. Or that time when sheet lightning lit the field, every color bent toward green, and barefoot on grass stubble, she found herself singing, mouth open to the sky.

MADAME
BUTTERFLY III

I look for the woman first, of course,
and then for the beautiful insect, but there's no figure here,
    nothing nameable

on this dark and woody ground.
        Three broad panels, to carry a hundred
layers of color and ambiguous

        shape. I think of Ophelia and Mary Jo Kopechne,
both glad to be out of it, and of Cio-Cio San bent
        over the seeking blade. The press

slams downward, and something
        strong and horizontal
advances out of the grain. A slow

        explosion. A brilliant flashpoint
trailing white-blue-gray,
        like paint spilled into a rushing stream,

or a kimono painted
        with winter hills. Something submerged,
but not lost.

        I think of my mother, face flushed,
hair damp, hauling drapery up to the rattling needle.
        Of Emma reciting

to her husband's child-face: This room
        is your room. You
are happy here. A red gash like a wound or a birth.

After Helen Frankenthaler, *Madame Butterfly,* 2000

APOLOGY

The two of us in our attic,
      double locks on the flimsy door, anti-war protests
         across town. My mother

in her raveled cardigan, my crib
      under the eaves. Between hands of solitaire,
         she reads a letter scored with black lines. It

can't tell her if he's alive. First and best, I loved
      her flecked and silvery eyes.
She taught me nine times nine, made my prom dress

from a thrift store hand-me-down,
      but that night with her husband missing—
         what did she have left for me?

Don't Talk Back for a lullaby?
      If I Should Die for a prayer?
         Is it memory or a wish—

her cheek against mine, our shadows merged.
      Hush, she says.
         Hush.

WE
ARGUED
ABOUT
SAINTS

I said: I'd sooner drink turpentine,
than sit through Sunday Mass, and Emilia said
I'd lost my faith
but I could find it again if I buried
a statue of St. Joseph in the garden.
I told her I didn't believe in saints,
except my parents. And she said:
Your father's a saint? I heard
he whips you with a willow switch.
No one talked about my father's hand,
hard across my face, not even my mother
spreading makeup on the bruises.
        I've driven a daughter
into her own wilderness, spent whole nights
shouting at the wrong man.
and I'm mostly sorry now
that I called Emilia a bitch.
I'm back to thinking about
ordinary people—distracted
by bad knees and payday loans—
but still saints. Like Emilia.
Like my father
on the day he taught me to fish.

AIR

Alone in my grandmother's
basement, I inhaled, and a Chicklet
wedged itself in my windpipe.

A funnel of light
gripped by a funnel of dark,
swung up and down the ceiling

while my whole unbelieving
body pushed and hauled and failed
to capture any thread of air.

Nothing else changed.
Upstairs, chair-scrape and a medley
of voices, a splatter of dog paws

on linoleum. Down here a drift
of yellow jackets murmuring night
into my ear, and all space

the woolly gray
of an army blanket. Somewhere
a key was about to click home—

and when it did, my father's belt
slashing my legs, minus
six Celsius, the man

who someday would love me—
all of it, would be given
to some other girl

not dying on this stone floor.
And then my brother found me, or
I fell into a chairback, or maybe

not, but anyway I went on
breathing, went on
forgetting the usual mysteries—

the words to Cohen's "Hallelujah,"
which is Andromeda, which
is Orion. And that room, already cold,

already underground.

THE
WIND
TELEPHONE

A farmer has planted a white telephone booth
on the headland facing the Sea
of Japan. He'd hunted for it through

all the junkyards of Honshu. Every week
he climbs the hill, dials the squat,
rotary phone, and speaks to his cousin,

the one taken by the tsunami,
along with his spare, elegant garden.
Every week the farmer tells the drowned man

about some new seed catalog, about the bitter taste
of this year's plums. Pilgrims come,
crossing his land. A woman dials an apartment

scoured away. A mother
passes the phone from child to child.
Lately, I dream I am the farmer,

sealed in some Ma Bell booth, blue and glass,
graffiti and wires, a black box.
I lift the broken receiver

and tell a certain man he was right.
We planted the mugo pine
too close to the house.

I WATCH
THE
CROWD

from the balcony—breathless—in love
with the pointillist brilliance
of restless bodies and the sharp,

dark face of a certain man,
his square shoulders, his crisp
white shirt. I bend forward

as if to pour myself into the pastel ocean
that surges below me. House lights dim
for the last act, but look—

that man's finger touches
his wife's throat, just here,
at the hollow. I'm not ready

for closets ordered by color,
by summer weight, then winter.
I'm not ready for the muffled room

allowed me, now I've been swept past
the years of the peach, the thin, brisk air
of mountains. If I can have only as much

as fits inside the circle of an opera glass,
then night after night,
I'll dream it all over again—

Joseph's slow smile, the lovely
breasts of Therese, the lost
Atlantic of your eyes.

After Marie Cassatt, *In the Loge,* 1878

WHAT TO DO IN THE DARK, II

Listen to the music your husband loved. Wear your grand-
mother's earrings.

Keep these treasures on your windowsill: a hemlock finger,
a fist of coral, the mummified paw of a fisher cat.

Polish the buckle from the belt your father used to hit you,
the tarnished eagle you saved from his dress blues,

and make a list of each day's most radiant cloud: stratus or
cirrus or cumulonimbus.

Over and over, tell the story of how the Gravely ripped the
rabbit's nest, bloodying the ground, and how your husband
brought you the one survivor,

he said only you could save it.

See? Your hands have changed. They are just like your
mother's.

To the bits from your windowsill, add a spool of red silk
thread and the beating heart of a wild rabbit. Place it all in a
Cherrywood box, and mark it: For my daughter.

OLD
AND
NAKED

She's got one swollen ankle cocked,
      like a petulant child made to pose
            and pose. But who makes Alice?

Only Alice. No truth left but spreading flesh
      mounded in a blue-striped chair,
            and so she chooses to record

the wreckage. Girl's waist, firm, young thighs
      lost in this mudslide. Her face
            a bitter, fallen face,

mouth pouting, cheeks jowly and flushed.
      But those clear eyes look out at me,
            one eyebrow lifted. She's familiar

with disaster—a daughter lost to suicide.
      Paintings a boyfriend cut from the frame
            to wrap the plumbing.

Now, her body dissolving, she'll do what she's always done—
      see what no one wants to see. Paint it.
            Leave it behind.

After Alice Neel, *Self-Portrait* at age 80, 1980

THE SISTERS

The one with silver eyes appeared
    in the basement playroom, my mother upstairs
        singing to the baby. Learn, she told me,
            the uses of loneliness, and when her wing

touched the ceiling, the old house
    wept. Later, someone ceased to love me
        so I gave my cheek to the gritty skin
            of the sidewalk. Men leaned over me.

Are you drunk? and a Sister with ruby eyes
    walked through them murmuring: Jasmine tea,
        December mornings. But on the night
            when the intravenous lines

pierced my husband's arm, the visitor
    had black eyes, no whites at all,
        and her kiss seared my forehead. She said:
            This death belongs to him. Let go.

In dreams, the one
    with my mother's silver eyes
        comes singing: Ashes. Ashes. We all
            fall down. August dusk

and she instructs me:
    Set the table. Set the table. Green
        apples and crisp brown bread. Wait
            by the unlocked door.

WHAT
WILL
BE
LEFT

Gravity, the Dead Sea Scrolls, and those styrene tubes
for wrapping string cheese. A long, unbroken wave

poised halfway across the Pacific.
For a soundtrack—the gravelly whisper

of a needle stuck in the last grooves
of the last vinyl. Stones will remain, the place

where Akhmatova stood near Leningrad Prison,
the slave shacks at Monticello, but not the vast

emptied-out maze of cyberspace.
Clocks will remain though not one person—

no, not even one—who can spot my distant face and say:
Oh, look, there she is. No frantic coupling

in the mountain laurel
at the back of the arboretum. No

little girl riding her Big Wheel. But still—for a while—
rosemary and thyme,

thunderheads like midnight spinnakers,
and the whale's skeleton

hung from the museum ceiling.
Each sculpted bone of his dorsal fin.

ACKNOWLEDGMENTS

Thank you to the editors of these publications where versions of the following poems first appeared.

Avenue Journal:	"Maybe They Will Drown Him"
Blue Lyra:	"Girls in Pictures"
Cider Press Review:	"The Wind Telephone" "The Sisters"
Crack the Spine:	"En Route, 1995"
Deranged Anthology:	"Old and Naked"
ELJ:	"Married Love. A Taxonomy"
Entropy:	"What Will Be Left"
Iron Horse Review:	"Almost the Fourth, 1980"
Magma:	"Cassandra and Me"
	"We Argued about Saints"
Paren(thesis):	"One Good Friday"
Pretty Owl Poetry:	"Night"
Salamander:	"Cold Thursday"
Slipstream:	"Bewildered" "I Can Hear the Night Train"
Stirrings: A Literary Collection	"Defiance in Girls"
Tishman Review:	"My Father Said He'd Teach Me" "Panama Sailor Boy"
White Stag:	"Madame Butterfly III" "Woman Prime"

I am grateful to a number of people who have patiently, brilliantly helped me to carry these poems forward from their scrambled beginnings. First my friend and writing partner, Erica Bodwell, who read every poem first and many times and never, ever failed to ask me the core questions and then refuse to settle for partial answers. To Emari DiGiorgio for her unique insights and tireless energy. And to the people who were there when I started—Judy Nugent, Joan Blessing, Art Ritas, and all the wonderful members of the Boiler House Poets. Finally, of course, to Tony and our daughter, Lisa. Without them I would have had so little to say, especially about love.